T0094845

Metastasis

Metastasis

Poems

by

Josie Di Sciascio-Andrews

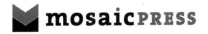

Library and Archives Canada Cataloguing in Publication

Title: Meta stasis.

Names: Di Sciascio-Andrews, Josie, 1955- author.

Description: Poems by Josie Di Sciascio-Andrews.

Identifiers: Canadiana (print) 20200377876
                Canadiana (ebook) 20200377949

ISBN 9781771615365 (softcover) ISBN 9781771615372 (PDF)
ISBN 9781771615389 (EPUB) ISBN 9781771615396 (Kindle)

Subjects:

Classification: LCC PS8607.I73 M48 2020
                DDC C811/.6b dc23

No part of this book may be reproduced or transmitted in any form, by any means, electronic or mechanical, including photocopying and recording information storage and retrieval systems, without permission in writing from the publisher, except by a reviewer who may quote a brief passage in a review.

Published by Mosaic Press, Oakville, Ontario, Canada, 2021.

MOSAIC PRESS, Publishers
Copyright © Josie Di Sciascio-Andrews 2021

Cover Design by Rahim Piracha

ONTARIO ARTS COUNCIL
CONSEIL DES ARTS DE L'ONTARIO
an Ontario government agency
un organisme du gouvernement de l'Ontario

We acknowledge the support of
the Ontario Creates

Funded by the Government of Canada
Financé par le gouvernement du Canada

MOSAIC PRESS
1252 Speers Road, Units 1 & 2
Oakville, Ontario L6L 5N9
phone: (905) 825-2130

info@mosaic-press.com

Dedication

For my mother, Iolanda Paoletti Di Sciascio.

She was the most loving, sweet, funny, humble, gifted and kind person. She was the light in my life and of all who knew her. She was taken from us too early from this horrible disease we call cancer.

"Per te, mamma! Ti voglio tanto bene! Ti difenderò sempre da tutto quello che ci ha voluto rubare l'anima e la vita."

Contents

Preamble

Metaphorically, carcinogenic, viral corruption threatens the world in an era of surveillance, monopolizing oligarchies and moral decay.

From an unexpected diagnosis, to the loss of a precious mother, to greed endangering our ecosystem, *Metastasis*, guides us poetically, through a dark, heartless underworld of invisible machinations.

Like Virgil leading Dante through the circles of Hell, it shines a light upon the rot of both the physical and spiritual disease spreading endemic, aided by artificial intelligence's net trap.

As above, so below, there is a weird energy tearing everything asunder.

Through the revelatory power of writing, philosophical ponderings and snippets of scientific data, this book illuminates us with emergent concepts never before tackled in a Canadian poetry collection.

Preface

From apes, to mimics of animals, fish, birds and insects, humans have succeeded in emulating the animal world for self protection and survival. From cars, to airplanes to hive-like skyscrapers and cities, our imitation capabilities have evolved into great civilizations. Presently, copying the behaviour of viruses, bacteria, carcinogens and parasites has given us a new edge for enhancement in the world of intellectual data mining. In stealth, invisible, the hacker, like a cancer, walks in and out of personal files to take what he needs to flourish. In our transhumanist era, artificial intelligence has made borders porous and dangerously vulnerable to attack, much like a body preyed upon by a malignant tumour.

Meta Stasis, as an idea for a poetry collection, ignited in my mind a decade ago, a period of time when my mother was diagnosed with terminal cancer and told she had ten years at most, to live. Simultaneously to this heartbreaking revelation, I discovered that my unpublished poems on my computer documents were being accessed and refurbished into prize-winning works by all sorts of writers, some of whom I personally knew. You can only imagine the sadness and the helpless grief that overtook me in view of these dismal circumstances. To stand exposed and defenseless against, what I can only call, the tragic undoing of my beautiful mom's life, as well as the unwelcome pilfering of my unpublished poetic work, were and continue to be two of the most painful experiences I have ever had to endure. The poems in this collection were born of this, tinged by an equally difficult backdrop of family and health circumstances. Except for the Wikipedia snippets of scientific facts and author quotations, I wrote each one from the heart.

The book is divided into three sections. The first part is my poetic response of pain and outrage at the realization that my computer network had been perpetrated by surveillance, akin to a body infected by disease. The poems in the first portion play on the metaphor of cancer, as it dupes the host's immune system, evades recognition and takes over the cells' command centres with the sole aim to self propagate by siphoning sustenance from its unsuspecting victim.

The second part of the book comprises ponderings about life, its meaning and the difficult task of continuing to hope and to live in the aftermath of losing a precious loved one to an insidious and incurable disease. These are poems that have had to come to terms with the nefarious effects of a deadly illness. They have shifted their focus from anger to sadness to acknowledgement of the universal finality of life. Love, grief, longing, bargaining and acceptance weave these words in an attempt to synthesize unbearable loss into some sort of ubiquitous meaning, as it exists in the context of the cyclical nature of life.

The third and final section of *Meta Stasis* delves into corruption and moral decay at the psychological, societal and political levels. In our global village, where mankind is now imitating the biological viral world through nanotechnology and surveillance, the negative repercussions of this transhumanist shift are coming to the fore, coincidentally with our current coronavirus pandemic, which has debilitated our lives and our economies. All the while, 5G technology has moved forth to band our planet with ever higher levels of radiation and surveillance capabilities.

They say poets are the antennae of their times. We are sitting on the shoulders of millennia of violence perpetrated upon innocence and recorded as history. For all our talking, philosophizing, politicizing, writing and fighting against wrongdoing and corruption, it is still here in the guise of empires, corporate conglomerates and top economies.

So no, these poems are not optimistic. They could not be if we look sober eyed at the world we live in. Although we have made so many scientific gains, the scourge of cancer is as real as predation in the food chain. So too are the ever present dangers of violence, theft, moral decay at every level of institution and government. One doesn't have to look hard to see a pervasive, narcissistic lack of concern for truth and boundaries allowing sociopaths to succeed via illegitimate means and image control. I wanted to look at predation of us by the invisible, lilliputian organisms and entities at the biological, virtual and societal levels. They are what will bring us down as individuals and as nations.

I do believe that poetry is a mirror of what is, as in dreams, a reflection of *animus mundi*. Through metaphor we can look at phenomena in the natural world and make some sense of its essence. It is with this spirit that I wrote *Meta Stasis*, the play on the word metaphor reiterating the morphological nature of our present world's number one killer. My poems are a rebuttal against disease, against surveillance and against sociopathy. This book is an outcry against wrongdoing, a manifesto of vexation and clear eyed realism which aims to highlight the odious, deleterious effects of unbridled selfishness, corruption and moral collapse.

The fly on the cover is a spirit animal, symbol of death, yet also of renewal. The humble house fly flits from corpse to corpse then contaminates everything it touches. It can spread disease, but it also cleanses the world of toxicity. At best, it allows for new growth and regeneration of life and goodness. It is my sincerest hope that science finds a cure for cancer soon, and that each human being afflicted by this horrible disease is healed. I also pray that as a human race we can stand up to laissez-faire legislations, which so far allow unbridled surveillance and gathering of personal data in saleable algorithms, without any legal repercussions. We cannot be pollyannaish about this. We must look at the facts head on to be able to be realistic. There is no cure. Cancer kills. Similarly, surveillance aims to funnel out our resources, personal, commercial and state secrets to disempower and dominate. Corrupted oligarchies aspire to supersede financially and to rule.

Les Fleurs du Mal, by Charles Baudelaire, resonated with me throughout the writing of this book. The collection of poems, *Flowers of Evil*, of which T.S. Eliot wrote, *"is an aggressive, even defiant rejection of liberal humanism."* I myself, wished to showcase the darker nature of the microcosm which endeavours to undo us for its own narcissistic, predatory needs. Eliot praised Baudelaire's *'awareness of evil'* as opposed to *"the cheery automatism of the modern world, that damnation itself is an immediate form of salvation"* he wrote, *"because it at last gives some significance to living."* It would be an understatement to declare our present world *'a wasteland.'* Against the optimistic, the normal, the healthy and the morally ethical, I wanted to give voice to the hellish paranoia and surreality of having to live in a body desecrated by terminal illness and a mind violated by computer hacking. I wanted to juxtapose to this, the reality of having to live in a world perpetrated by corporate greed, war, ever expanding and frightening technologies and the resulting environmental and societal catastrophes of our times, where *"the ceremony of innocence is drowned"* and where Yeates' *"rough beast, its hour come round at last, slouches' still, 'towards Bethlehem to be born."*

Josie Di Sciascio-Andrews
February, 2021

Raising a Fly

I am raising a fly
whose wings are made of gold.
I am raising a fly
with eyes of fire.

It brings death
in its fire eyes,
it brings death
in its hair of gold,
death rides its beautiful wings.

Inside a green bottle
I am rearing a fly:
no one knows
whether it drinks,
no one knows
whether it eats.

It wanders in the night
like a star,
it inflicts mortal wounds
with its red splendour,
with its fiery eyes.

There is love
in its fiery eyes,

METASTASIS

its blood glows
in the night,
and the love it brings
in its heart is glowing.

Nocturnal insect,
fly, carrier of death,
inside a green bottle
Ever lovingly I nurture the fly.

One thing is certain:
no one knows
when I give it a drink
when I give it.

by José Maria Arguedas, 1965
From "The Invisible Presence" Mosaic Press 1996

Part I

"Loathsome canker lives in sweetest bud."

William Shakespeare

The Deathless Hoyle Bird

It never dies,
but only goes to sleep,
after which, fire
destroys it.

An egg remains
however, and from that egg,
a full grown hoyle
hatches anew.

Syntax

Breaking syntax
Breaking code
Breaking a whole number
Askew
Syntax askew
Broken bits
Of inverted meaning
Subvert subvert
Tie tongue
Tongue tied
Unleash tongue
Tongue lashings
Glib
The snake
Confusing heart
To rationalize
Disparate parts
Nonsensical
Groupings of information
Datum byte bitten
An acrid apple
Software malware
Entering divinity
To separate perfection
Coherence dichotomy
Decompose decompose

Compost composition
De-construct destroy
Annihilate nihilism
Take wholeness
Back to zero point
Before creation
Undoing uncreating
Death

Malignant

the opposite of benevolent & benevolence
from the latin male + gnus = born evil
mutations in whole genome sequencing
in situ = contained in one location
anaplasia = on formation, a condition
whereby cells lose their morphological
characteristics of mature cells
and their orientation with respect
to each other and endothelial cells
lack of differentiation is considered a hallmark
of aggressive malignancies

Outside the Circle

Nobody understands
you live outside the circle now
in this surreal, suspended
purgatory waiting to fall
down to the infernal pit
to dissolution

you wait for the gods
the universe
the specialist
to pull out the tumour
entwined in your entrails

white bells of bindweed
the universal essence
in you taking you back
into its' folds like a mother
tucking you back into her womb

it enters an open door
of you somewhere
you didn't know you had
and through the roof of your house
of safety, your house
of life, it forces you to evacuate,

to retreat into the old corner
of despair

you adulterated,
your inner sanctum
perpetrated, desecrated
peopled with the malignant gaze
of a million crab eyes

privy of you
of your loves
of your hopes
of your dreams
of your secrets
now fodder for their grip
on self preservation, growth

you: their road to immortality
their only purpose, to groom your words,
your story into their own meaning
you, nothing but soil, *engrais*
for their seeds to germinate unimpeded
which you, palliative
will fight in vain to extirpate:
terminal cancer.

The Invisible Presence

'that it had made a living off of you
with its' taciturn conniving

a larva queen pupa
securing its' own
house fly kingdom

and like a fly,
it defecated on the beauty

of your flesh succinctly
taking the sum

of your life for its' own
horrific sustenance

reviled insect
flitting
from corpse to corpse

with its' incessant
repulsive, living buzz

"Resistance is futile. You will be assimilated."

Star Trek, The Borg

"I have found it amusing, and all the more pleasant because the task was more difficult, to extract beauty from Evil."

Charles Baudelaire from "Les Fleurs du Mal"

Annexation

It was like lifting up
a chunk of mossy soil
to discover a world
of insects busily decomposing
the substratum of what you assumed
to be your stable ground
your terra firma -decomposing you
your cells like lines, ingesting them
appropriating you, your life
unafraid that you may discover this,
unflinching, impudent, animalistic

Metastasis
(adaptation)

Definition:
a change in position,
state or form; the spread
of a disease producing agency
as cancer cells,
from the initial or primary site
of disease to another part of the body;
also, the process by which
such spreading occurs;
a secondary malignant tumour
resulting from the metastasis

Etymology: from Latin *transition*
and from Greek *methistanai*
= to set more at - to stand

Wikipedia

"As above, so below. All things have their birth from this One thing through adaptation."

Hermes Trismegistus from "The Emerald Tablet".

Cancer

Subverts the order
Of our DNA's syntax

It takes
Our body's coherence
Back to chaos

She undoes us
To create herself

Erodes our form
To feed her need

She is ultimate ego
The ultimate narcissist

Forges ahead to fame
And perpetuity

With her selfies & stolen goods
A wanted criminal here, yet at large

Untouchable

Spreading quantum
Unkilleable, ad nauseam

METASTASIS

Replete with accessories
Accomplices, apps

Pages of trademark trails
Rewritten in botched up DNA

Each chance she gets, she flashes
Her finds, flaunts them, like a dog peeing

Territorial, brainless on a fire
Hydrant, eager to mark her heists

When will she die?
Can we fight her?

She has taken and takes
So many. We will die first

Somebody please
Find a cure!

Grenade

cancer mass
in the shape
of a grenade

black, green and blue
pink, purple, bloody red

you take all
I ever had

a pool of iodine
waiting at the bottom
of a blade

I slide down

a sliver in the brain
this pain

this life spun
by love

undoing, undone
my name

never the same

Skene

Agar dish
Or stage

We are dropped in
At birth

Stand unaware

Then move and splay
Into possibilities

Destinies

Live Bottom Red River Systems

What if you thought
You had me first?

But I was just pretending
Playing dead

And you

Unaware
You would be next

Hacking into
Your own
Ill fated end?

An Invisible Microscopic Lattice of Interstellar Points

She has lodged herself inside you.
A matriarch in a seedy neighbourhood.

Her head is large. Fat. Frayed
Black mess of adipose tissue.

Skin, tooth, enamel, follicle
Membrane weaving madly

Your stories into glib spin.
A mass production of child labour.

Replicating. Replicating.
Here. There. Everywhere.

Your organs are now planets
Or continents she stitches

With arteries between peripheries
Gorging on a limitless supply

Of sustenance. You. Thrombosis
Of convergence. Ugliness

Of a fat lady singing last
Before the show is over. Anomaly

Grows rampant. Feigning absence.
Invisibly devouring edible people, you.

Hollyhocks, lips and wine in symbiosis
With guns, fragments of bone, scar marks.

A blob of horror like the one in the film
Named "The Thing." That came from outer space.

Rolled down the city streets in mucous blebs
Swallowing everyone. Swelling larger to grotesque.

Her colossal success in profits alone.
How many cells she deactivated to feed herself.

Mutely. Gargantuan. She gained its famished fame.
Obese with words. Without making a sound.

For decades she was there, acting all benign.
A tumour. Complicit. Eating in the dark.

A sumo wrestler. Pretending to be innocuous.
Growing. Appropriating. Displacing. Killing you.

Biding her time. A macrophage with insect wings
Waiting to burst out of her membrane

And shoot out her flawed, warped seeds
Reproducing herself like an evil queen.

Claiming her non existent beauty
In some metaphorical mirror.

Cruel, old witch queen. Eating.
Expanding. Presuming to be cleverer.

Smarter. Outwitting you out of your body.
She opts out for immortality.

METASTASIS

Oh great delusion! Her body's a conglomerate.
The eye of a fly. Her platinum head, jet black ill will.

Death mongering. The calculated praxis
Of a real estate developer getting rich

From rezoning your picturesque small town
With tacky monstrosities of baroque renovations.

Her face, skeletal. Sociopathic cheekbone
Structure. The sullen, olive opacity

Of those photos of the dead. Veined
With irony, scorn, broken pink capillaries.

Wrinkled. Pocked. Rosaceous.
Black beetle deploying tendrils

Into the suburban landscape of you
To secure herself a place

Outside her anorexic, red insect enclave.
Malignant face. Fragment of sin.

I am Sputnik

Fragments of sin
are part of me.

Appellate jurisdiction.

Blooms will sweep
My heart clean.

Light carrions.

Light of life passed away.
Cast away.

Malignancy.

Cleansing

In the end
There will be choruses

Of darkness echoing
In cold, damp abbeys

Sound spiralling up bat-like
Towards concave ceilings

Emanating vibrations
Into the star-lit night.

Human voices
Like swarms of flies

Will grow in darkness.
Their egg-like larvae

Cleansing the world
Of death's useless rot

In the universe's endless quest
For renewal. Orange lilies

Will bloom their burnt amber centres
Like the yawns of savage lions

In the parching August light
Of another life season.

Wind will blow their powdery pollen
With dead locusts' ashes.

Desiccated centipedes. Bones.

Life's forms unraveling through time.
From dust to dust.

Obsidian

They came in droves.
In calculated sequence.

A procession of insects
decomposing a corpse.

Each set of bug species, timely.

In predetermined order
At cessation of breath.

They took everything.
Like colonialists or capitalists.

Each man for himself.
Secured his position.

Immigrants, squatters, refugees.
Colonies. Cloning. Moving in.

Made fodder of your dreams.
As if you didn't matter.

You: native, wild, uncivilized.
Inexpert in their art of cunning.

Some took a piece of this.
Some took a piece of that.

They took your best lines.
Your best words.

Built mine shafts
Down the spirals of your DNA .

Aimed for the gold in you.
Your soul code. Heart code.

They took all their arms could carry.
The full measure of your love.

Too little. Too much. Enough.
Shucked it all of your life story.

Erased your mother
From the laundry lines.

Your father from the music.
Your children from the beaches.

Just the words, please!
They said.

Your life, minus you.
The essence of you. *Thank you!*

Your body parts sequestered, dying
For a predator's lack. Sacrificed.

They reinvented your hands, your eyes,
Your face. Poured wax in the muscles

And sinew of your limbs, your bones.
To prop up their own epic

METASTASIS

Momentous fame. Baroquely.
One hit wonders, number ones.

Each warped cell monstrously amoral
As a sewer rat gnawing at your toes.

They kneaded you amorphous
Displacing order into necrotic globs.

Narcissistic gods, avid for more.
They saw you as food.

More code to spawn
Their inanities in more locations.

Out of obscurity, once marginal,
You will suddenly notice the burgeoning

Scallops of them fattening
Now in central nodes

In major ports of your circulatory system,
Lands you imagined yours, invaded.

Mere substratum now. Desecrated
For their pablum, formless kind to replicate

Malignant diasporas,
Until there will be nothing left

Of your geography to pillage.
That's when they will fold and bluff.

Take you down in a kind of coup d'état.
Suicide bomb themselves

To detonate the universe of you.
Your future life's emergence

Denied to feed their polyglottal hunger
And they will conjugate, to supersede immortal.

Faulty conglomerates of error
Photocopied ad infinitum,

And for a time, they will parade, vacuous
Yet full of you in the front rows of greatness.

But though, they will go down in the grave with you
When you die, their kind will persevere to thrive

In someone else's life. Hierarchies of darkness, hacking
Anew their deformations into the symmetry of light.

Again they will pack shapeshifter-like masses
Of sense into meaninglessness. Shibboleths

Proliferating their number one killer brand of seed.

Now this particular cell

Suddenly turns barbarous.
Turns against you.

Defective.
It replicates in error.

No more idols
But me. It states.

You have reached the outermost
limits of your time.

She refuses apoptosis.
Leaves that option up to you.

The crab takes root.

Unlocks the combination
Of your marrow's code.

Splays out at will.

Your future stalled now.
Vertical.

Corrosive egg.
Queen of tentacles.

Black haired Medusa growing fat
With her paraphernalia of doom.

Pods

From unknown destinations
With an encoded will
Of drive to outlast
They embedded their nucleus
Inside the command centres
Of a cell: this nucleopeptide
Borg, master of disguises.

Shot out microscopic
Cannulas in science
Fiction horror mode.
Suction cupped itself
Onto veins and blood lines
Aspirating codes of ribonucleic
Acid. Extrapolating sum & substance
To replicate modified versions
Of themselves, the body's tags of truth
Removed. DNA bared
Of meaning, like tissue
Brought out under the lights
Of a lab by a scientist's latex
Covered hands. Formaldehyde.
Stench of death. The data
Gathering of eyes, yellowed
Flesh in suspended state
Of rigor mortis.

Once her stygian head jiffy-pops
Like the swollen cranium of a daddy
Long legs, her host syphoned
Out and inert, this evil nabob
Assures herself in cosmic mirrors
Of her unsurpassable beauty. Stardom.
Sends ax men with hatchets
To shred the membranes

Of metaphorical snow whites
Living their lives, oblivious
In quixotic enchantment
En - chant - ment
In the media res of their stories
Unaware of any evil doing
Singing in the midst of blitzkrieg
While big C gorges herself
To her limits, from their cells'
Blood. Emits poisonous spores
Of herself to the rest of the recruits
Propagating. Rewriting
Original creation.
With her own
Distorted assumptions.
Ironies. Disses. Attributes
Of the parasitic
Survival strategies
Overwriting
Overriding
Wreaking havoc
On the form
Of previously ordained
Order.

A hell raiser
Chaos maker
Anomaly of anomalies
Daughter of failed apoptosis
Fallen angel

Rogue
Black-marked blight.

She is a mutant mutation. Covert
Ardent eavesdropper of her host's core.
She has the black box.
She multiplies in impertinence
Shooting quantum chemical messages
To distant topologies of the body
She has invaded. Black melanoma
Berries sprout up in her image.
Flowers of evil.

Flowers of Evil

Darnel
Zizzania.

Malelingue
Evil Tongues.

Gossips
Spreaders of ill will.

Les fleurs du mal.
Children of sin.

Zizzania zigzagging
Courte-pointe of threads
Like candy floss mildew
In hedges and empty flower pots
After a humid night.

Tiny black spiders
In a cottony tangle
Of white, eliciting
Disgust. Horror and ghosts
Of bluebeards walking ominous
Out of the water
Towards you.

And that the dream
Is not a dream is stunning.

A mind in collision
With Dawkins' selfish gene
Theory. Abraxas
Deploying protein
Tentacles throughout
The fibres of your life context
Obliterating it for its own
Purposes. Kneading it anomalous.
Undifferentiated.

A cancer mass.
Human tissue with no name.
No purpose. No story.
Just text in a Word Doc.

A file of information
On a desktop. Without reference.
To be reused and recycled
At the cellular level.

Like yesterday's lunch.
Like compost.
Like the young pigs & livestock
Transported in trucks on highways
For slaughter.

"He's an Oscar Mayer Wiener."
Contaminated with chemical sulfites.

And while you ponder
This cataclysmic catastrophe,
This black octopus
That's made its way
Into one cell of you,
Is already manufacturing
Replicas of itself, globally

At quantum speed
With bits of you inside
Its own brain now
To disarm your defences.
Grow huge from you.
Grow popular
While you recede
And die.
For what will seem
To her like an eternal lifetime.
This Cleopatra wannabe, posing
Biting her annoying, swollen lip.

Like cities all over the map,
Nodes will appear exponentially

At once. Burgeoning melanomas.
Cities of them, razing
Branches of lungs and brain
Tissue to the ground.

And that this beast
Will grow hungrier as it grows.
Eating like crazy.

I read a book
Called 'The Triffids'
About flesh eating plants
Once. Eating their victims
From a bedroom window
As they unsuspectingly slept
In their beds.

I was so revolted, yet
I couldn't put it down.

The pods.
The pods.

I remember a dream
My sister had, where giant ones grew
On our driveway.
Their large green mandibles,
Heads of spiky, comb-like
Teeth. Waiting to gulp
Someone up. Ah yes!
Gulping the gullible. Me: Gullibility!

They will make you think it's a dream hallucination!
Sorcery! Madness! Except these pods
Are dark souls. They're alive. They're real.
Some of them are fair or white haired.
Their faces seem beautiful.
They pretend to be socially conscious.
They smile while they thieve. Deceive.

They want your blood.
Your cypher. Although
They do not like you, per se.
Their name is greed. Is fame.
They will outlive you.

Imperialist mindset. Retrograde
Belief in ranks and cast systems.
Husbandry. Pioneer Seigneurie.
Primitive throwbacks with cannibalistic
Urges. Visible in their determined
Animal stare of supremacy
In their 'with a vengeance'
Shrewd smirk of their mug,
To kill their prey. Swallow it whole.
Dominate. Dominus Dei. Dominion.
Supremacist contempt for those they deem
Their minions. Poisonous black tarantulas.
Carcinogenic. Annexation points.
Expunge! Expunge!
The body's immune system
Has tried and failed.

Now, this dainty Mrs. Claus
Look alike, Satanic empress
Has taken over the control tower.
She reigns supreme.
Like a bruise. A clot.

Inside her childless blue door,
She puts out books of you.
An industry of books.
Replicas of her barren, childless heart
Into the world. Replicas. Replicas.

Replicas. Of you. Of everyone.
Of everything. A dark pod.
Pods everywhere.
Malignant. Propagating.

Alive for a while.
But when you die
She will die too

Leaving traces
Of herself in virtual
Soon to be forgotten print.

A nondescript, amorphous glob.
The stuff of black and white horror
Films. Blame it on bad parenting.
Blame it on greed. She is "The Blob."

Tumour

I scribe the tales of old
The caustic bubble

Of the melanoma
Angioblastoma curr

The tail end of nasty
Supernova trailing
Its last leg

Dark pubescent roil
Of un-remittance

Missing the
Centre point

A throne of dust
Incarnate

Destroy, remake effigy
To seethe

Likenesses of death birds

In its' own image
Its' laws in every prong

Its macabre smile
A colonizing death grimace

Mediocrity squandering it
Heiress privy sweeping
The streets she never owned
Sweeping, sweeping the data

Arachnid in the bananas
A morass of tangled words
Bipolar verbiage necrosis
Necropolis in the Chiquita box

Diagnosis

Ten years or more.

It's jarring to discover
They were spawning cities
And galaxies inside you.

That they had somehow found you
Living in the mundane obscurity of your days.

Honed in on the command centres
Of your cells, hacking into your files.

Documenting everything. Documenting.
Accidents. Loves. E-mails. Poems. Conversations.

Access found through a LAN door
By the probe of their technical hired hand.

Once access was gained, you unawarely blood-let
Yourself to their successful growth.

A conglomerate economy of hungry fanged cats
Spun spires. Such as is customary of hardwired predators
Of good men and sparrows.

As if they were imperialists or capitalists,
They took your code like pelts or tusks or oil.

Trampled and revamped the cartography
of the original map of you.

Tabula rasa, your flesh a fertile Klondike
To feed their larval selves.

And that they didn't work alone! A demolition crew
Contracted and paid in concerted calculation

To feed off the metaphor of you.

They too are light.
Light light.

They are alabaster flowers.
Look how they bloom!

Their microscopic clusters
Accrue in drone-like stalactitic mainframes
Into the ground of your being.

That essence wrapped in skin
You assumed to be you.

No more ego bound than the earth
You walked upon since birth.

You - light permutations
Upon the waves - rags of clouds
Dispersing in wind currents -the love that spun
You into being -no more, no less
Than their infinite need
To take root within you.

They re-impose their own order
Upon your fertile estuaries.

Everything teems with its own meaning.

And even as you sit this morning
Pondering your impending demise,

At this decaying picnic table
Mould, micro-organisms, moss, lichens
Are feeding off the ageing wood.

Cleansing. Taking solidity back into the void.

The universe's invisible hands grasping
Every object. Every beautiful thing.

Pluto carrying Persephone to the underworld.
Marrying her unto itself.

These cancer cells have hacked into your meaning.

Soon they will drag your youth into the darkness.
To re-envision their own sense.

Misconstruing you and refurbishing
Your days into new hierarchies of being.

So too beneath your feet
The grass grows tall with weeds
And crickets are hatching in the clover -

Your elbows lean on rotting wood.
Emerald borer locusts, spider webs
And fungus mushrooming out of a dying tree.

Diagnosis II

It always begins with an unexpected diagnosis.
The culprits having embedded themselves
In some compilation of your body's network.

And to them it didn't matter who you were.
How nice you were. What face you had.
All they wanted was the treasure in you.

Those little nuggets of gold they could sift
Out of you to sustain their oeuvre, inflate
Their sagging sails with, to point their egos

Towards glory. The only thing you can be sure
Of is that you will be incorporated. No two ways
About it. The corporation's corpus will make you

Part of their foundations.
You will see bits of you glowing,
Standing out like radioactive isotopes

In the neoplasms' latest, winning tomes.
Tumefactions. Aggressive. Progressive.
Metastasizing. Incurable. Terminal tumors.

Progressive

It made an industry of you.
Silently hacking into your mind.
Surveilling your every move. Listening.

A bolex lens recording
Your most private moments
Exploiting for its own
Perverse malignity,

The life you believed
Your own.

You say: "I wasn't born for this"
As it continues to feed
From your veins.

It wins.

Soon your name will shine
On the stone of your epitaph.

(adaptation)

Apoptosis = from the Greek 'apo' = away from
        and 'ptos' = falling
        is a process of programmed cell death
        that may occur in multicellular organisms
        biochemical events lead to characteristic cell changes
        (morphology) and death

Morphology = is a branch of biology (and language)
            dealing with the study of the form and structure
            of organisms and their specific structural features

Cancer changes the morphology of our cells from their normal, native, benign ability and necessity to diversify into: brain, heart, muscle, veins, blood, bone etc. Cancer subverts the morphology and once the command centres of the body's normal cells are broken into and warped, cancer creates amorphous cells with no diversification. These chaotic cells continue to grow unstructured and take up space where normal organs are/were. Eventually their growth causes pain by pushing on nerves and it starves the body of the host, by syphoning out all the nutrients and blood supply.

Apoptosis

Shucked of story
The words are lymph
Blood for your spin

Disembodied disambiguation
Ambiguous space
For emergent concepts

Unrelated to maudlin passions
Elemental air, water, fire, clay
Molten, cooled

To amorphous stratum
Scaling, flaking off,
Splintering in profuse

Wind particles, cloud formations
Infusing your hungry skeletons
With form. With infinite light.

Malignancy
(adaptation)

the opposite of benevolent or benign
from the Latin 'male' + 'gnos' = bad born aka 'born evil'

Mutation

in whole genome sequencing

In Situ

contained in one location   locus = place, site
locare = to talk, to speak

Anaplasia

on + formation = a condition whereby cells lose the morphological
characteristics of mature cells and their orientation with respect to
each other and endothelial cells * lack of differentiation ensues -is con-
sidered a hallmark of aggressive malignancies -multiple sub-clones

Histology - Cytopathology

malignant, malignity, ill will, virus, virulent, malign, vitriol, malevo-
lent,
maleficent, spite, rancor, malice, venom, execration, desecration, evil

Cancer

Something has invaded us
and rewritten the secret
recipe of our cells.

Once it has caused disruption
to enough of our cells,
our natural defences
or cell spell checkers

fail to function properly
and our bodies succumb
to their infiltration.

Carcinogen

for whatever reason
the cell's replication program
is altered - a glitch in the program

it is now believed the cell
is altered by a virus
deploying into its network

Modus Operandi

First, you had to get yourself lodged
in high places. A central location
with access to the brain
of the operation.
Like a university creative writing
chair position or presidency -an overseer
of literary contests
become privy to all the words
all the codes -a librarian technologist
helped you -I know her -she has cancer too
karma is a bitch

Neutralization

They tied your hands.
Turned you around and made you kneel.

It's easier to kill someone from the back.
Everyone looks equal. Nondescript.

And execute you they did. One by one.
In line. With the divinity of your eyes

Facing pavement and wall. In the name
Of themselves. Of industry. Fill in the blank.

Blank. That's what you were to them.
A blank canvas upon which to re-write

Their own story. Appropriation. Subjugation.
Neutralization. Annihilation.

I wonder if cancer cells are like that.
Non-malevolent really. Like coyotes.

Just famished and self-serving.
Howling their hunger in packs. At night.
Creatures like us, adapted to survive.
Just born that way.

Like men hard done by poverty, abuse. Amoral.
Fighting and stealing their way to a meal.

Just trying to make a buck. Hermit crabs.
Slugs. Dissidents. Ambitious delinquents.
Goldilocks trespassing in somebody else's house.

Metastasis

Imagine the world
As a body. Human.

Stretching out its arms
Through a page

Or the vault of a chapel.
Visualize the yearning

Of mankind
In search of appagation.

That invisible pivot
Of mathematical accuracies

We call the perfect number.
Beauty. Form. Apex.

Now, imagine the black
And white memory

Of an old retro reel
Of a Super 8 film splaying

The screaming, naked run
Of a Japanese child

Bereft of everything
Alone in black and white

Running away from an atomic blast
Rearing its ugly mushroom
Head behind her. Iconically.
Fat Man on Nagasaki.
America silencing the world

For world supremacy.
Little Boy at the top.

Ebola

a threaded loop
so simple
yet so complicated

God's boy scout knot
dad's tie
the one you couldn't learn

the scarf technique
the latest trend

Cat's cradle
Fibonacci sequence
Incarnate

Spaghetti couldn't loop
itself so well unaided
by life's current, mind

to articulate itself
into a hacking weapon
of entry into a body's cells

a spiral in diagnostic
specimen photography

virions varied flexible
filaments with a consistent
diameter of 80 nanometers

varying greatly in length
although their genome
is constant and degree

of twisting negatively
stained virions
magnification: approx. x60,000

some filamentous virions
fused together end to end
the perfect noose

hook inside eyelet
of thread pulled tight
knotted firmly

sewed twice
in the underside
of your epidermis

to keep its ghastly fibrils
safely inside

Virus

The video shows how a virus
infiltrates the cell.

It's like opening
a locked door
with the right key.

Viruses
turn your cells
into tiny factories
that help spread
their disease.

A flu virus
can trick
a single cell
into making a million
more viruses.

It only takes one
virus
particle
to infiltrate
our body

before millions
are replicated
unwittingly
by the nucleus
of our cells.

Thankfully
our bodies are home
to 100 trillion cells,

meaning a million viruses
is just a drop
in the bucket.

We come equipped
with a healthy
army/ aka immune system
capable of killing
off any invading
viruses it comes across.

virus (n.)

late 14c., "venomous substance," from Latin *virus* "poison, sap of plants, slimy liquid, a potent juice," probably from PIE root **weis-* "to melt away, to flow," used of foul or malodorous fluids, with specialization in some languages to "poisonous fluid" (source also of Sanskrit *visam* "poison," *visah* "poisonous;" Avestan *vish-* "poison;" Latin *viscum* "sticky substance, birdlime;" Greek *ios* "poison," *ixos* "mistletoe, birdlime;" Old Church Slavonic *višnja* "cherry;" Old Irish *fi* "poison;" Welsh *gwyar* "blood"). Main modern meaning "agent that causes infectious disease" first recorded 1728 (in reference to venereal disease). The computer sense is from 1972 (https://www.etymonline.com/word/virus)

Strangely & yet interestingly
The Latin word for man is *Vir*

Are we *viruses* upon the Earth?

"Your body is the piece of the universe you've been given."

Leah Pearlman

How Do Cells Become Cancerous?
(adaptation)

"A healthy cell does not turn into a cancer cell overnight.
Its' behaviour gradually changes as a result of damage
(from a virus?/ a carcinogen?/ radiation?) to between 3 to 7
of the hundreds of genes that control cell growth, division
and life span. First, the cell starts to grow and multiply.
Over time, more changes may take place. The cell
and its' descendants may eventually become immortal,
escape destruction by the body's defences, develop
their own blood supply and invade the rest of the body.
A cell is continuously receiving messages, both from its' own
genes and from other cells. Some tell it to grow and multiply.
Others tell it to stop growing and rest, or even to die.
If there are enough "grow" messages, the next stage
of the cell's life starts. In a cancer cell, the messages to grow
may be altered or the messages to stop growing or to die
may be missing. The cell then begins to grow uncontrollably
and divide too often. Every time a normal cell divides, the ends
of its chromosomes become shorter. Once they have worn down,
the cell dies and is replaced. Cancer cells cheat this system.
They retain their long chromosomes by continually adding bits
back on. This process allows them to live forever. (Cells from
Henrietta Lacks, diagnosed with cancer in 1951, are still growing.)"

https://www.ncbi.nlm.nih.gov/books/NBK279410/

61

Invading the Body
(adaptation)

"Most normal cells in your tissues stay put, stuck to each other
and their surroundings. Unless they are attached to something,
they cannot grow and multiply. If they become detached
from their neighbours, they commit suicide, by a process
called apoptosis, but in cancer cells the normal self-destruct
instructions do not work, and they can grow and multiply
without being attached to anything. This allows them
to invade the rest of the body, travelling via the bloodstream
to start more tumours elsewhere. MISSING CHECKPOINTS.
Every time a healthy human cell divides, it copies all its genes,
which are bundled up into 46 chromosomes. This process
has several checkpoints to ensure that each cell gets a near-perfect
copy. But in a cancer cell, these checkpoints are often missing.
The result is chaos: parts of chromosomes may be lost,
rearranged or copied many times and the genes are more
likely to acquire further mutations. Some of these may allow
the cell to escape other checking and repair mechanisms."

https://www.ncbi.nlm.nih.gov/books/NBK279410/

From an original copy to chaos.
Cancer creates '**sigint**' = non-sense, non-meaning

Why are cancer cells so powerful?
(adaptation)

All the cells in your body usually work together
in a community, but if a cancer cell acquires a gene mutation,
that makes it multiply when it should not, or helps it survive
when other cells die, it has an advantage over others.

Eventually, the abnormal cells acquire mutations in more genes,
causing uncontrolled growth. These abnormal cells, like hackers
have a competitive advantage over normal cells.

This is like natural selection in evolution, where a species
that produces more offspring has a better chance at survival.

Why don't cancer cells die normally?

In normal cells, gene damage is usually quickly repaired.
If the damage is too severe, the cell is forced to die.

An important protein called P53 checks for gene damage
in normal cells, and kills them if the damage is too great
to repair.

However, in cancer cells, these mechanisms
are defective (as in a computer with no firewall).

Cancer cells usually have an altered P53 protein, which does not work properly, allowing the cancer cells to survive, despite their dangerously garbled genetic/*poetic* material.

https://www.ncbi.nlm.nih.gov/books/NBK279410/

Cancer Cells, Narcissists & Sociopaths

Boundary testing and hoovering.

Like cancer, narcissists, sociopaths
And otherwise toxic people
Continually try and test your boundaries
To see which ones they can trespass.
The more violations they're able to commit
Without consequences,
The more they'll push the envelope
To see how much they can hoover out of you
Without you knowing. Ultimately taking you down.
That's why survivors of emotional
As well as physical abuse
Often experience even more severe incidents
Of abuse each and every time they go back to their abusers.

All abuse, like cancer, is about silencing. Is about killing.

Eugenics

The human genome project.

In 1990 scientists started a vast
international project that aimed to decode
all of our genetic information by 2003.

Since we are now in 2020,
it has been long decoded.

That was at the human body level.
In the metaphorical body of text level,

I discovered the decoding happening
Since about 2003.

I had them at 'pupa'.

Trolling

as they searched for the most luminous
                fish in the planetary glow
of my dream, upon seeing all their kindly, lovely faces
                      I was awestruck
and thrown back into the darkness of my canoe

black ink night   cavernous water
            Who would have known that death would be so sweet?
      That friends would lead me to it   presumed friends
    Their social berried hearts no better than contraband gun barrels
aimed with precision and calculation at the centre of my chest

        Falling back   astonished   at discovering who they were
              still,   for a while   I reeled in the moon,
        entangled as it was in a net of fangs and distant stars
          good memories mirroring on waves in spite of evil
                        toxic wastes
        reflections of beauty and light somehow, still washing
ashore

Legion, gestalt of the damned

they found fertile land
and must have gasped with joy
smiled to themselves

embedded their lilliputian claws
into the mast cell's membrane

it was all good
too good to be real

another dumb Goliath to be taken
down, stoned by the slingshot
of the nth invisible needy foe

with a Napoleon complex
Sadistically slaying people (for self defence?)
like David in those biblical verses

"Cancer cells can grow faster, adapt better. They are more perfect [d]versions of ourselves."

Siddhartha Mukherjee in "The Emperor of all Maladies"

Part II

"This place where chancres blossom like a rose."

Malcolm Lowry

Quantum Sparks in the Tabernacle

The light enters and I remember who I am, why he is here.
Here in this room, I have bounced from particle to wave
Then back again. This room is my life. Contained in it
The theory of everything in my allotted chronology.

This space. So Hadron collider-like, collapses the observed
Into the equation of myself. Light bound in materiality
Of skin, armour, gold-prayer beads and knives to stave off
Threat. It could be you or anyone, sitting on this death-bed baldachin.

Curtain pulled back around the altar by the white
Clothed arm of an angelic nurse, comforting us
In our final hour. Gabriel announcing our birth,
No sooner warning us of The Second Coming.

Here is the world summed up. Born to its unending
Legacy, in the blink of an eye, faster than light
We arrived to it unwittingly, this crux in space-time.
Like meteors and stars, irrupting onto the stage,

Clumsy and unknowing, our form bursting forth
Through water -slapped by a midwife's hand to tick
For years like a clock in the tedium of an antiseptic room.
Our body, mere measurement of Pi -Vitruvian mystery

METASTASIS

Encompassed in ratio of circumference and diameter
Squared -alive at the centre of this cathedral tent.
This is my tabernacle for the sun.
I am holier than holy nothing. Just another packet

Of life quanta propped up on a theatre of shrouds-
Re-enactment of sacrificial goat immolated to the idol
Of the day. See the damask cloths. See my pale face. Its halo
Cap. Beyond the nave, up in the chancel pulpit.

I am the quintessential incarnate book -a rebus
Of words -the calculus theorem solved, with zero sum.
Alla luce ausurum, ut partier ab pulvis.
Animalia of tails and fangs -vestigial appendages hound,

Bewilder us & biological hormones pulse
On towards our own dark, doomsday clocks.
Now here, we drop our shoe at the sound of twelve.
Irrupt in reverse in a rattle of breaths,

Blue domino effect of genetic cards. Red heart
Folding back the abacus of us. Each switch
Turning off the trillion suns we believed were us:
Segments of light made manifest between two points.

On this canvas, expanded equivalence between Gabriel
And the Christ -in azure, copper ochres & carmine,
Our genome's laid bare -mere script of DNA
Chromosomes of anonymous humanity in a never ending chain.

This room is a pop-up book of you and me
Replete with everything we saw -gathered
In time, compressed to two dimensions now.
Still reel frame of our near-death, life in review.

Reptilian, then mammalian -untidy & holographic
Selves inch in within the data of our evolution, although
We sweep the evidence under the bed, they are born,
They lust, they reproduce, they die.

Metastasis

And while we dream and reason, the monkey beasts
Emerge to tempt us back to hunt and gather our survival, Even as
Jesus, fallen from his cross, now enters, lance
In hand, to claim us from the sacristy back to his tomb.
I am the circular cell and the infinite wall is closing in.

* lines in Italics from 'The Watcher' by Jorge Luis Borges -'Selected Poems'
Penguin Classics, p.72

(This poem was inspired by Bosch's painting "Death of a Miser"
-I wrote it when my mother was dying with cancer.)

Oncology Department at Credit Valley Hospital *

A young woman sits in the waiting room.
Leafs through *Glamour* and *Time*.

I don't know her exact diagnosis,
but she's wearing a chemo scarf.

She's sipping on a pastel pink straw
from a super sized Styrofoam
cup, of what can only be a prep solution.

If you could just change the backdrop,
you would swear she's at McDonald's.

Fast food. Check!
Chemical preservatives. Check!
Formaldehyde leaching from plastic
packaging; GMO's. Check!

It all makes me think of Jesus
at the last supper,
and the way he was betrayed.

The scourging. The thorns. The nails.
The bitter vinegar they offered him
on a sponge in his final hour.

The story of his murder neatly staged,
re-told in twelve sequential stations. Process
of prognosis after diagnosis and then the step-
by step theatrical stage, set.

As if always, after the breaking of the bread,
a handing over for anointing follows

in a ritual of scientific protocol.
And we comply. That's all we can do.
Ticking each box off on the clipboard,
completing every step to our undoing.

Supernova

Mamma is sleeping in her bedroom.
She sleeps every time she takes her pain killers now.
The pain is getting worse. Unbearable.

She never used to sleep so much. When I came over
She was always doing something: gardening, cleaning, baking,
Going shopping. Going to church. Having coffee with her friends.

I can almost feel the particles of foreboding in the air of her house.
An eerie light has replaced the usual sunlight through the sheers.

I miss my mother even though she is still here. Still alive.
Cancer is taking her. Although I'm in denial, my mother is dying.
She will soon be gone and leave an eternal void in her body's place.
A void so unexplainably painful within me
There are no words to describe it.
Just tears. Just swallowed, choked emotion.
My love for her with nowhere to go.

My mother is the sun.
She is a star.
A star-sun in my universe.

Soon she won't be here.
Energy will empty out
Of all her cells and merge

Back with universal consciousness.
Energy. Space. Nothingness. God.

I can feel it in my being.
The biggest cataclysmic catastrophe
Of her life. Of my life.

My mother is dying.
She is imploding.
She is my sun collapsing inward.
Her light is so strong, but it will shatter
And disperse everywhere for the rest of my whole lifetime
The brightest, hottest luminosity
In this third last act.
This final drawing of our story's curtain.

The First Christmas Without You
(for my mother)

There will be no turkey this year.
No candied cake. No celebration.

Now that you're gone
The feasting is outside the house.

Snow falling on the familiar landscape.
Sparrows feeding on your lawn.

Berries red in the thorn hedges.
Squirrels thriving in the yard.

As of late, so many missing cat posters
On hydro poles. Coyotes and foxes

Killing anything smaller
And weaker than they are,

In blind, narcissistic predation.
Ferocious, like the invisible

Illnesses decimating us
All on the inside.

A Painting of Canaries on a
Sewing Machine by a Window

My mother's sewing machine
Rests still now

Beside her bedroom window
With the lace curtains.

Tiny yellow birds have nested
In her garden.

Small feathered suns
Camouflaging in the yellow

Daisies. Burnt amber petals
Flying off with wind into the blue.

Everything is alight with colour.
Intense with the chatter of birdsong

On another summer morning
Without you. Alive. Alive.

Everything alive.
Everything conspiring

To accentuate your absence.
The hollow empty ache within me.

This yellow brick house you took flight
From. An empty nest teeming with you.

Darkness

So dark
Without end

Consciousness steps
Tentatively forth

Moonscape
Arid, frozen

So cold
Breathing halts

A paper world, snow
Gleaming and the moon

A face
Of worried physiognomy

Of this leap we take
Finding ourselves

In hyperboles
Of nothingness

The days
Opening up

In their infinities
Their repetitions

Filibuster

When the rains came,
they were filled with omens,
faces of feral dogs.

Like bandits,
well versed

in the arts of piracy
Thieving the echoes of our souls.

Distant Blue Flowers

You think you can see the world in a bit of dust
And you envision paradise in a measly weed.

You try to grip the infinite with your fingers,
Relatively. In sixty minutes,

You attempt to gather the eternal.

But your i-phone rings
And the dog needs to piddle.

You log onto Facebook.
Scroll for a while.

You're sick
And late for work.

Beautiful blue flowers
Sway in someone's post.

Food Chain Fairy Tale Or
How to Teach Children About the World

"You're eating me
Alive! Stop!" Said the prey
To the predator, and any other
Animals that could listen
And help. But they couldn't see.
Didn't want to. Busy
As they were, climbing
Trees with better friends.

They hated the prey
For speaking up.

"So negative!"

"Such a troublemaker!"

"Be gone!"
They concurred.

Her plight
Ruined their day,
So they turned away
While it happened.

"Better her than us!
They reasoned.

Some took tufts of her fur
Left on the ground
For their nests

And felt lucky.
Some took bits
Of her paws and tail.

Then they focused
On nice things and nice friends
So they could have a good day.

Amalfi, like Casoli on Steroids

and yet ...
everything
brings me back
to the places
that formed me
these houses
these windows
these doors
these archways
and lamp posts
everyone I knew
is missing though
been replaced
by other people
people I don't know
my heart leaps
an octave loop

back and forth
through memory
through time
tears bloom
from my eyes
from the roots
of grief nostalgia
breeds deep

this place
brings me back
always always
I am a child
growing old
walking with you
away from you
towards you
the world everywhere
an oyster
of us

Part III

"Are we growing an economy or a cancer?"

Alaura Weaver

"Growth for the sake of growth is the ideology of the cancer cell."

Edward Abbey

"To hasten growth is to hasten decay."

Lao Tsu

They Have Calculated all the Angles

Secret documents reveal
how energy companies use
fake "Grassroots" pressure
to get what they want.

Leaked documents expose
shady tactics behind PR
push for even bigger
Canadian pipelines.

Spy
(adaptation)

"A nation can survive its fools
and even the ambitious. But it cannot survive
treason from within. The traitor moves
amongst those within the gate freely,
his sly whispers rustling through all the alleys
heard in the very halls of government itself.
He rots the soul of a nation, he works secretly
and unknown in the night, to undermine
the pillars of the city. He infects the body
politic so that it can no longer resist.
A murderer is less to fear."

Cicero

The Matrix
(adaptation)

"I'd like to share a revelation that I've had
during my time here. It came to me
when I tried to classify your species.
I realized that you're not actually mammals.
Every mammal on this planet instinctively develops
a natural equilibrium with the surrounding environment,
but you humans do not. You move to an area
and you multiply and multiply,
until every natural resource is consumed.
The only way you can survive
is to spread to another area.
There is no organism on this planet
that follows the same pattern. A virus.
Human beings are a disease, a cancer
on the planet. You are a plague.
We are a cure."

Agent Smith,
From 'The Matrix'

Prague

The wheel of freedom
Is disappearing

He set himself on fire
He was screaming

But the music kept on playing
He was taken away by security

The individual has very little power
To make changes

Pointless

One gangster changes
Into another gangster

The silence of bystanders
Reiterating, solidifying the horror

All of them complicit by inaction
Unwilling to help for fear
Of self repercussions

Sins of omission
Blameless witnesses
Co-creators of Hell

In an Age of Corruption
(adaptation)

"People who live in an age of corruption
are witty and slanderous; they know
that there are other kinds of murder
than by dagger or assault; they also know
that whatever is well said is believed".

Friedrich Nietzsche

Anonymous' Motto

We are legion.
You don't see us.
We are everywhere.
We do as we please
With you.
We are your doppelgangers.
We can see you.
We have a beautiful view
From our square.
Une Belle Vue
From our panopticon.
We own you.
You're virtually a pigeon
As in the urban dictionary sense
In the proverbial Truman Show.

Red Queen
(adaptation)

"We will rise up
Red as the dawn."

Victoria Aveyard

Tower

Don't look for gold on Wall Street.

There, indefatigable Brinks trucks
Ironclad corporate hegemonies.

Relentless, on our highways, big rigs
Transport America's iron & metal
For infrastructure and sewer grates.

From their steam, in sub-zero winters
Outside the city banks, the homeless sleep.

In icy sunrises, their sacred exhalations
Lift up like brief hopes. Freeze silent.

Priapic obelisks in the mouth of the metropolis
Grow visible through clouds of noxious smog.
Its pearl chipped fangs hustling.

Inside a front of gargoyled, stately spires,
Hanging like sausage from the plaster,
Bats fatten in the belfry.

Grids

The grids are here
The grid makers have gagged the earth
With lines north and south
East and West
Wires cutting through oceans and continents
Longitudinal, crisscrossing latitudinal sphere
Invisible wire nets, internets
Capturing fish out of water
Suffocating the gills of the world
Gasping for oxygen
Under the tubes and pipes
Of smoking factories, railways
Highways, chemtrails, perpendicular grids
Of metal, glass, binary steel
Bolted, welded onto fleshy growths
Of botanical, animal forms protruding
From lips, eyes, earth's skin
Bionic tumescences dangling
The last outcroppings of separated minds
Creating antiseptic, linear scapes
Where dinosaurs are hearts
And towers crumble
Where men blow up
Without pain

Without sadness
And humans are mannequins
Remote controlled
By celluloid gods

War Believers

These are the ones
That would hesitate
At the thought of ending wars
As if you were taking away
Their right to breathe.

"What? No killing?
It's what we live for.
The essence of a man."

These are the ones
Who swear
By honour
Righteousness.

These are the ones
Who obey
Rules and rulers;
Who stick to truths
As sharp as blades,
Passions as red
As homicide.

Postmodern Chaos

We converge on the centre

Around the void
We form a mecca of hopes

Concoct futures
Reinvent old histories.

In the heart of the city's crucible
We become new entities

Reshuffle our foreign selves
In the amniotic foam of new possibilities

This agar dish we will multiply on
Replicating our old selves

The way we used to be
Before the split of body from tribe

Before we found ourselves cut off
Within the world's plurality

Filled with the deep ache
Of scission

Cutting umbilical cord
Of our genetic soul

Wounded with the invisible scar
Of our humanity out of context

Out of place
Another breath within a million breaths
In the giant lungs of the global city

Accruing in the relentless peregrination
Of the earth's disparate peoples

Exchanging their flesh for capital

Definition of "Malignant" from the Webster Dictionary as an adjective pertaining to a person / *plus my own definition from experience of this beast* *(adaptation)*

Very serious and dangerous.
Can cause death.
Very evil
Evil in nature, influence or effect.
Injurious
Passionately and ruthlessly malevolent.
Aggressively malicious.
Tending to produce deterioration.
Tending to infiltrate, spread deleterious rumours
In order to terminate fatally.
Synonyms: bad, bitchy, catty, cruel,
Spiteful, malevolent, nasty, vicious,
Malicious, hateful, mean, virulent
A serial bully.
Haughty. Boastful.
Faking goodness.
Glib.
Sociopath.
Narcissist.
Malignant narcissist.
Psychopath.

Personality Disordered.
Liar for self gain.
A suck up to people higher up.
A denigrator of people lower down,
Unless they serve some purpose.
Attaches him/herself to central
Most important managers/ pivots.
Manages well, their surface image.
Well liked by most
Who are used by & don't know

His/her knivings.
Thief. Again for self gain.
A murderer. Ditto.
A total jerk.

Nothing New Under the Sun

We emerge once more from sleep
Privy to the world
With all its pulsing strivings.
Its' hungers, griefs. Again sunlight
A menagerie of shapes
Usurps imagination
Solidifying all we wished for, dreaded.
Parapets of doubt, invisible shadows.
The faceless world fills its' sail.
Grows strong from our meagre sustenance
Of loss and longing. Of hope. Embeds
Itself and of its own ghosts makes bread.
Multiplies phantasmagorias
For good or not. Allineates
Itself with kindred essences.
Galaxies of dust.
Enter our code.
Deactivate. Silence.
Feed to fruition. Bloom.
Bubbling to the brim
Of beakers with hypothetical assumptions.
Equations. Calculated science.
Les Fleurs du Mal. Les Fleurs du Bien?
Good for you? Toxic?
You will know them
By their fruits.

A Way of Life
(adaptation)

"When plunder becomes a way of life
for a group of men in a society,
over the course of time
they create for themselves a legal system
that authorizes it and a moral code
that glorifies it."

Fréderic Bastiat

Two Thoughts
(adaptation)

"The greed of gain has no time or limit
to its' capaciousness. Its' one object
is to produce and consume.
It has pity neither for beautiful nature
nor for living human beings.
It is ruthlessly ready
without a moment's hesitation
to crush beauty and life."

Rabindranath Tagore

"Greed's worst point is its ingratitude."

Seneca

Disease

the earth's crust has a skin disease
a case of microbes infecting its crust
and that sickness is man

the city is a pathological process
fray masses of urbanoid tissue
homogenized masses, scabs

these disparate phenomena seen
together with the speed
at which they are proliferating lately,

gives us an overall theory and hypothesis
that provides an explanation
for these changes as cancer-like

Individualism/ Capitalism
(Every man for himself)

And then, maybe
There was never
Any malignant intention
At the heart of these cancer cells

They too, pushing forth the limits
Of their own emergence

Light manifesting its code
In permutations of some inherent cypher

Their quantum nodes
Spreading throughout the body

The geographies of the body
Like interstellar space stations

Connection dots on a splayed map
Of Earth all gridded up at night

Points lighting up exponentially
Like births per minute

Or death bleeps on heart monitors
Human activity on a graph

The horizontal lines
Calculating fleshy outgrowths

Accruing like living stalagmites
The vertical registering their impact

> "To seek out new worlds and new civilizations; to boldly go where no man has gone before."
>
> *Star Trek*

Meta Stasis
Mass Migration
Intergalactic Space Travel
Orbital Stations
Cosmic stepping-stones
The possibility of life on Mars
Jumping from cell to cell
From planet to planet
From galaxy to galaxy
Send our trash into the sun

Adaptation

No sooner had they been born,
They had hungers, needs.

They staked out territories.
Preyed on any available food source.

For their own survival.
Their own proliferation.

Unaware of the horror
They would sow. The devastation.

Their self continuance
The only central preoccupation.

Everlasting life sequence.
Everything else peripheral
Black space.

Buffering consumers from crop failure

If I should die
Pick the pupil from my eye.

Bake a pie of crows
And pigeons from my flesh.

Take my body
Take my blood.

Hold it up to the sun
So you may proclaim

Me as your code.
As yourself.

A Flowering Presence

The body coming out of its pink wrapping
The corpse manner of this death.

The skeleton, fat & sinew
Ancient monument
Intestines peat bog.

Worms, Celtic Gods
Terrorism, good science prophecies.

Mass migration heart anvil
Imperfect past, past perfect.

Syndrome

Atemporal, a-local
You could be anyone anywhere

A sartorial sleuth
Collating seasons, lines

Feelings, states of mind
Consciousness inchoate

My father's death could be
Your husband's or aunt's demise

The sentiment the same
Although the names and places different.

Effete, you give yourself up
To science. Analytical technology.

You loved the snake. Took his advice
And ate the apple. Know it all.

Forget about God. You top him
Now. Take everything you can.

Earth is so passé for you.
Just oil and money, warheads.

A disposable, portable paradise.
Should you get sick, you will

Have yourself cryogenically
Frozen. Your sperm too.

Frozen and sent off into space.
You'll be back. Three hundred years from now.
Oh joy!

Seagull

No angel
Scavenger
Eats anything Predatory
Lives on a beach
In plaza's parking lots
White grey plumage
Sociopathic stare
Hungry yellow beak
Short neck, stout bodied
Thin legs, wide webbed feet
There is no taming of this shrew
Beast of prey's voracious hunger
Costumed in white feathers

Palimpsest

Annexation of Crimea
Or any place
For self
For profit
Data
Black Box
Extract
Information
Twice removed
You write a world
Without a heart

Google

We are a mass.
Data is the new oil.

When we wear brands
Ethnicity is irrelevant.

There are no borders.
Countries are passé.

There is no skin. No psychic boundaries.
Anyone can hack anyone anytime anywhere.

And why not? The apps are not illegal.
After all, there is no "I" in team.

And what's good for the team is good for the gander?
So, let them walk through your brain and take what they want.

There is no you anyways. We are all one.
Imagine there is no country and no religion too.

Insects and birds behave with hive mind. Murmuration.
We humans just thought we were unique. Ego trip.

Individuality has become a misnomer.
Hydra would not contest.
Many heads are better than one.

You deserve it!
Just do it!
You're #1.

For marketing purposes
You're the best!

But don't delude yourself.
You're no more special
Than the last casualty

Or the next customer.

You are the consumer
And the consumed.

You're just a momentary blip.
One post on one Facebook page

Quickly read. If you're lucky
Liked or shared, then soon forgotten.

One post on a perennially rotating
Social media wheel. A mouse. A rat.

An experiment spinning in a cage.
For research. Profit. Art.

You will look great in someone's trilogy
Of Hell. As a sinner, a poet or a pilgrim.

A customer: you. One unit. One cubit
In a data graph algorithm.

One point in a growing megabyte
Within the global village universe.

This feudalism gone spatial.
Gone berserk.

Black Friday

I have waited for you
to pass by me, pass over me
like everything else in my life

the sales, the fanfare crowds
the regalia of signs and lights
new clothes in mock silk

galas of perfunctory ceremony

blanketed in worn flannel
in place of donkey skin
I rub my face and hair with ash

revelling in the servant wing
refuge from the dark ventricle
of profit's upper chambers

"Black Friday!"

go on now, with your caravan
of lies, jesters and goods-
leave me here by the fire

my eyes are closed, I dream
I am a cat curled up for a long sleep
wanting nothing, nothing but peace

Metastasis II

That you had to take my life
Says volumes about your swaggering
Weapon: jeer of an assassin.
Your lack of an eye for beauty
Or form at the height of your career
For all your sputtering, convoluted
Efforts at domination, just a pimple
A cauliflower floret expanding
Its ugly brain desecrating loveliness
Dreams, life, you: a self appointed axe
Entering anyone's cranium, heart, lung
Or visceral tissue to simply reinstate yourself
Like a flag post on someone's moon
You, with your lilliputian catapults
Slinging your stones in the cyclopic
Vistas of the ones you vilified
For your own feeding, feeding
In your mad frenzy to nowhere
You replicate your vulgar order, your asymmetries
Onto the pre-existing equilibrium
Of someone else's life poem
Killing the blood
That fed you
That same lymph

Taking you too
With my corpse
Into the the closed coffin
Of that dry, ironic nihilism
You exhale as your god

Without justice, rulers are just successful robbers "

Augustus

The New Normal

You will get used to it.
One day, you won't even remember
The way it used to be.

Slowly. Incrementally,
The new reality
Will enter
Your present.

In small doses
At first.

At times forced
Drastically upon you
By sudden external shifts.

Proverbial crises.
Man-made turmoils.
Tectonic rearrangements.

Then, yesterday's normals
Will begin to fade
Into explainable histories.

Words to restring
The frames of a film.
Frames of yesterday.

And soon you will get used to
Your aging reflection.

The customs you had to give up
To acculturate in your new country.

The people you had to leave behind.
The ones who died.

The small percentage of radiation
In your drinking water.

All those nuclear tests
They did since world war II
Morphing the DNA.

The polar caps melting. Venice drowning.
The disappearance of the rainforest.

Australia burning. Dictators posing
Globally as democratic leaders.

The children they're maiming in wars.
The innocent people rotting in jails.

The wars. The money
They're making off the wars.

The plastic refuse choking our oceans.
Animals of your lifetime going extinct.

The stalemate of right and left.
Rationalizations with nothing ever changing.

The internet. Hackers. The dark web.
The fake news. The fake everything.

Monsanto. Pesticides on your apples.
On your cornflakes. Stored in your fat.

And yes, you will rationalize it.
Minimize its gravity

To survive.

A thing you wouldn't be able
To bear, should the undiluted truth
Hit you at full force.

You, like a seagull
On the polluted shore
At the city's outskirts.

Blinded. Lame.
Pecking at oil drenched algae,
Stones. Making do

With an injured, malfunctioning wing.
Hovering in semi-flight
Over the corrupted world,

Sunlight shining on the garbage
Dump of a tainted planet.

War

Yankee
Extreme
Extortion
Komatzu
Kamikaze
Reckless
Carnage
Carnage

The Harbour

The animals have fled
This God forsaken place.
Run away for cover
Into the remaining hideouts
Of forests, oases.
Humans too
Have run back somewhere
To the safety of their houses.
Away from the deathly reminders
Of rusted steel. Paranoias
Of dystopian futures.
Orange-red sunlight
Infuses a fetid blight
Into ozone empty
Turquoise skies.
Vitriolic
Caustic blue
Un-potable lakes
Once bearers of life,
Now mere cauldrons
Of industrial fluid.
The in and out cleanse
Of the city's saleable steel.

War on the Planet

At this very moment
Someone is dying.

Another Christ
Is staggering in a city alley
Or behind a barbed wire wall,
In a desert
To his own Golgotha,
That ever present place of skulls.

Random is this death.
Multiplied to the nth power of blood
Under the light of a relentless sun.

At this very moment
A child is being born.
Bundles of hope
Swaddled in innocence, while
With their strategic plans and war scrolls,
Corporations and heads of state
Wait to harvest him away
From his crib of dreams and lullabies.

At this very moment
A poet is writing
Of men dying,
Of children hatching in mine fields,
While the scornful plot their ploys of gain
Unaffected by poems or human tears.

Fake News

Today we are obliged to be realistic
To invent yet another rhyme.

We know the rules and proclaim the scientific.
Today's the day we have to be diplomatic.

Our world is old, yet new and hectic.
They're perfecting the atom bomb

While we prattle in vowel-chime,
And saying this has made me feel politic,

My dearest president. My darling mastermind.

Mosque

We escaped into the sweltering darkness of an alley. Footsteps of armed soldiers echoed on the humid cobblestones, feverishly reflecting the illumination of the mosque beyond the rooftops. The light led us to the monolith. From mullioned windows, telescopes scanned the city. High-tech devices with weapon capabilities. We hid from their beams into a shadowed stairway down to the riverbank. In the twilight, we witnessed people being carried off by the current; children waving their arms, drowning. And an old oracle slumped by the edge, watching. *It happens everyday now.* He cried dolefully. *It's the end of times.*

Pacific Heart

Earth's own Mare Nubium
The other side of the known.

A heart pumping ventricle.
Intergalactic melt of eons.

Where does the light go
In its deepest dark depths?

Cold, the world turns and drops
Into hues of blue. Rocks like a ship,

As fragments of amaranthine
Moon astound our smallness.

Petroleum, gas, pearls,
Salmon, shellfish.

The cunning take it all.
Call it survival.

Laugh in the face of wilderness
Though temperature records break.

Magellan's peaceful sea
Rattles in oceanic debris.

Breathes heavily from the hypoxia
Of nuclear tests & oil spills.

But relentless, the sea forgives.
Nurses its wildness.

Tonight, on the rising waves
The stars are shaking.

Portal

I awaken to the sound of wind rushing north from the lake
Reiterating its cries of urgency through my slightly open window.

Across the morning roads I can hearing it dragging its guttural echoes
Hushing to a hissing sibilance in the tangle of winter trees,

Ransacking the powdering of newly fallen snow from pine branches
Obliged to bow to its relentless force like the frosted paws

Of some benevolent animals, fanning the entrance of my musings
Into the enchanted wonder of the world.

Snow has fallen on the snowy path.
I can see it blowing from the thatched roof across the yard,

Pulling my thoughts to the memory of a period armoire
Filled with coats and furs.

Something about hiding out from war. A secret passageway
From the safety of an upstairs study into the wilderness.

At once I understand C.S. Lewis conceiving Narnia

And below the snow-covered blue spruce on my lawn,
A quintessential squirrel, the colour of bark
Darts across the frozen grass to its refuge.

METASTASIS

Invisible to my naked eye, evil and goodness
Lurk, rife to manifest in characters yet to be known.

Inside a castle's four walls, an ice queen
With a frozen heart is dreaming dystopian futures.

Infinite universes of infinite suns
Implode then coalesce

Into forever new chess boards of destinies.

And in the deserts, good lions
Are struggling to survive
The scourge of greed and science.

Half men like sphinx, like centaurs,
Alone in their lofts, are plugging in
Their human selves to technological devices.

Half animal, with gods and myths demoted,

Heaven and hell mere remnants
Of archaic imaginings, guarded

By the three pronged head
Of profit, taser and gun.

Narnia is here.

I can see it vividly this morning
Like those images that pop up into relief

From a sea of dots
When you've been staring at them for a while.

Outside my window it re-emerges
With its flurries and light posts,

Beckoning with its boughs of fir
Pointing up and out

To the pale peripheries
Of this house, this street.

The world fading to invisible atoms
Of light and darkness

Taking on the human physiognomies
Of good kings and despots

With their respective armies
Of horses and rooks

Cast to refashion the fate of our time
With the same old rhetoric

In new words and new clothes.

Pandemic

"The doomsday clock
Updated announcement
Reads 100 seconds to midnight.

'Humanity continues to face
Two simultaneous existential dangers-
Nuclear war and climate change
(Washington, D.C. * January 23, 2020)

That are compounded by a threat multiplier,
Cyber-enabled information warfare,
That undercuts society's ability
To respond. The international security
Situation is dire, not just because these threats
Exist, but because world leaders
Have allowed the international
Political infrastructure for managing
Them to erode.'   (https://thebulletin.org/doomsday-clock/)"

(March 28, 2020)
I write this.
We now have a coronavirus -Covid-19 Pandemic.
We don't know if it's a naturally occurring viral epidemic
Or a man-made bio-attack. With propaganda, fake news
And erosion of trustworthy reporting, due to probable
political gag orders and media control,

We are in danger of not surviving.
Life as we knew it has ended.
The economy has come to a halt.
The streets are empty.
Everyone is in quarantine
Kept in check by amber alerts
Governmental rules and check-points.
The virus kills and spreads.
Multiplies daily, exponentially.
It takes the weak, the old.
It has no mercy.
Technology gone awry.

Coronavirus,
An invisible planet
Of hooks
Velcroing themselves
To the pneumatic
Softness of the lungs.
To drown us.

Thousands have died
Already. Dying daily.
We don't know how long
This will continue,
If it will ever end.

Once you get better,
The virus is still inside you.
It can re-activate
At any time.

We are done for.

This is a catastrophe. Societal collapse.

Empires will be brought to their knees,
While others will rise. Cryptocurrency.

Metastasis

The psychopaths of the deep state
And the dark web are counting on it.

While people die, they pillage to thrive.

The doomsday clock has not been updated
To make room for Covid-19.
Once the small hand hits midnight,
We may no longer be here to tell the time.

If anyone survives, at that point
It will become the task
Of a new civilization to upkeep.
Let's hope the children make it.

Goodnight good people of Earth!
May you all be safe!
Over and out!

Jurassic

The machine gun-like helices
Of a copter on Isla Dublar
Rescues what's left of them.

Try to imagine yourself
In the Cretaceous period.
Tyrannosaurus Rex, animatronic.

Darwinian, bird of prey binocular
Vision. Roar of elephant, tiger
& alligator in synesthesia.

Thundering footsteps of sequoia
Falling to the ground. Gallinimus
Limbs torn in smithereens,

The simulated grunt of a dog
Attacking a rope toy.
The billionaire philanthropist

With his team of genetic scientists
Had envisioned paradise
In a wildlife park of cloned dinosaurs.

Resurrected life-size reptilian
Specimens with DNA from mosquitoes
Preserved in amber. Genetic

Information from bullfrogs
Added to modify & fill in the gaps.
All female to prevent breeding.

Computer generated prototypes
Enhanced using industrial Light & Magic

On the American set, while Spielberg,

In Europe, filmed Schindler's List.
A sixty-five million dollar
Marketing campaign that grossed

Nine hundred million in revenue.
In its third run, surpassed one billion.
During the storm, as night falls,

The park's computer programmer,
Bribed by a corporate rival to steal
Dinosaur embryos, deactivates

The security system, allowing
Him access to the embryo chamber.
The power goes out. Electric

Fences are deactivated.
The vehicles become stuck.
Tyrannosaurus Rex, the star

Of the film, climbs over
To attack the group. *"Decipher
The code to reactivate security!"*

They cry, retreating to the bunker.
Flinching at the severed arms, legs
& torsos they step over in the hallway.

The raptors ambush and kill Muldoon.
The broken shells of dinosaur eggs
Give evidence of breeding. West African

Frogs morph sex
In a same sex environment.
Now they are everywhere.

The last few humans board the helicopter
To escape the island. Grant
Decides not to endorse the park.

Acknowledgements

Oncology Department at Credit Valley Hospital. This poem was previously published in *Another Dysfunctional Cancer Poem Anthology,* edited by Priscila Uppal and Meghan Strimas, Mansfield Press, 2018. The anthology was selected by Chatelaine Magazine as one of the top Canadian poetry books of 2018.

    The Harbour. First published in *Sea Glass,* Espresso Bar Publishing, 2008.

    War on the Planet. First published in *Sea Glass,* Espresso Bar Publishing, 2008.

    Mosque. Judge's choice award in the Spring Pulse Henry Drummond Poetry Contest in 2019.

    Selected for publication in The Blue Nib, an international poetry journal in Ireland in 2020.

    Pacific Heart. First published in The Banister. Judge's Choice Award for The Banister's Poetry Contest, by the Canadian Authors Association, Niagara Region.

    Portal. First published in *Letters from the Singularity,* In Our Words Inc. 2015.

Readings

The Art Bar, (Toronto); Urban Folk Salon, (Toronto); Howl Radio U of T, (Toronto); Writers and Editors Network, (Toronto); The Heliconian Club for Women in the Literary Arts, (Toronto); Columbus Centre Book Fest, Librissimi, (Toronto); Knife Fork Books, (Toronto); Italian Cultural Institute, (Toronto); L'Alliance Francaise, (Toronto); Books and Biscotti AICW Event, (Toronto); The Ontario Poetry Society Readings, (Toronto); Poetry & Prose, (Oakville); Studio 89, (Mississauga); The Oakville Public Library Local Authors Reading and Video, (Oakville); The Oakville Literary Cafe, (Oakville); The Burlington Public Library Local Authors Event, (Burlington); The Griffin Prize Poetry In Voice Sessions, (Oakville); Oakville Galleries Poetry Sessions, (Oakville); The Artis Launch, (Oakville & Mississauga); Ottawa Italian Festival of Poetry, (Ottawa); Namashoum Persian Radio on The Canadian Poets Series, (Ottawa).

Biographical Note

Josie Di Sciascio-Andrews is a poet, author, teacher and the host & coordinator of the Oakville Literary Cafe Series. Her latest book of poems *Sunrise Over Lake Ontario,* was launched in 2019. Her previous poetry publications include: *Sea Glass, The Whispers of Stones, The Red Accordion, Letters from the Singularity and A Jar of Fireflies.* Josie's poetry has been shortlisted for the *Malahat Review's Open Season Award, Descant's Winston Collins Prize, The Canada Literary Review, The Eden Mills Literary Contest* and *The Henry Drummond Poetry Prize.* Her poetry has won first place in *Arborealis Anthology Contest of The Ontario Poetry Society* and in *Big Pond Rumours* Literary E-Zine. Some of her poems feature on *The Niagara Falls Poetry* website. One of her pieces was included by Priscila Uppal in *Another Dysfunctional Cancer Poem Anthology,* Mansfield Press, *in 2018,* rated by Chatelaine Magazine as one of the best Canadian poetry books of 2018. Josie is the author of two non-fiction books: *How the Italians Created Canada* (the contribution of Italians to the Canadian socio-historical landscape) and *In the Name of Hockey* (a closer look at emotional abuse in boys' sports.) Josie teaches workshops for Poetry in Voice and for Oakville Galleries. She writes and lives in Oakville, Ontario.